What Now, Courage?

What Now, Courage?
Grieving Judy
Poetry & More

By Alice R. Friedman

CHB Media, Publisher

Copyright © 2011, 2019, 2021 by Alice R. Friedman

All rights reserved. No part of this book may be reproduced in any form or by any electronic or mechanical means, or the facilitation thereof, including information storage and retrieval systems, without permission in writing from the author except by a reviewer, who may quote brief passages in a review. For permission contact arf603@gmail.com
and put permission in the subject line.

ISBN: 9798533311816

Revised ©2019, 2021 by Alice R. Friedman

Acknowledgements:

I want to thank those who have given me education and inspiration: Bruce Aufammer who insisted I write poetry, Jamie Morris and Mary Ann DeStephano, for their creative environments. A special "thank you" to Susan Lilley whose workshops sharpened my craft and for her willingness to review *What Now Courage?* Finally, Poetry Ensemble of Orlando: Russ Golata, Leslie Halpern, Estelle Lipp, Oral Nussbaum, and Bob Osborne, I appreciate your encouragement, great critiquing and fun.

"Big Bird" first appeared in *Remembering Faces,* an anthology of women celebrating women, by Palettes and Quills 2008; "Teddie's Ashes" in Chronicle 2001, Prize-Winning Poems by Seminole Community College; "Beginnings" and "Faith" in *Poetry to Feed the Spirit, Poets of Central Florida,* by CHB Media published, 2009; "Maternal Lament," "Mother," "Split," 'The Garden," "Beach Walk," and "The Last Gas Station," in *Connections: A Collection of Poems by Poetry Ensemble of Orlando,* 2008; and "High Noon" Originally appeared in the *Orlando Sentinel* online. "Forgiving Mother" earned the Editor's Award 2014 Thomas Burnett Swann Poetry Prize Competition appeared in *Revelry*.

*For Rachel and Amy
who gave me courage*

About the Author

Alice R. Friedman's articles and essays have won honors in National and State competitions of National League of America Pen Women, Florida State Poets Association and Mount Dora (Florida) Writers Competitions. Her poetry has appeared in several anthologies and on the Orlando Sentinel and WMFE-90.7 websites. In 2014 Alice won the Editors Award in the Thomas Burnett Swann Competition of the Gwendolyn Brooks Writers Association of Florida for her poem, "Forgiving Mother" which appeared in the journal Revelry. She has served as secretary of both the Florida State Poetry Association and the Orlando Chapter.

A former journalist, Alice retired in 2002 to concentrate on creative writing. She is the proud mother of two and grandmother of four.

Contents

Beginnings 11
I Wanted 12
Beach Walk 15
Learning Jazzercise 16
Ethiopian Princess 17
On learning that I am an introvert 18
GramIrene 19
Mother 21
Forgiving Mother 22
Teddie's Ashes 23
Summer in the Hamptons 24
Split 25
Maternal Lament 26
A Haiku for you two 28
High Noon 29
August 18 30
Big Bird 31
A Letter from Karen 32
Leaving Fred 33
Leaving for a Meeting 34
The Garden 35
The Last Gas Station 36
I Stopped at Athena for a
   Hummus/Taboule Pita 37
The Train 38
Faith 39
I'll Probably Die in Florida 40
When I am Gone 41
The Wall 42

Grieving Judy

Author's Comments 43
Fifteen Days in February-March 2015 . . . 45
Reading Alice Munro 46

Overwhelmed and Observing 47
What I Remember 48
And Beyond 51
Heaven in Travis County 53
May 29, 2015 55
Judy's Ashes 56

And More Poems

Lake Lily 58
Chucho 60
Storm Warning 61
April 21, 2015 62
Hoodeet 63
Alienation 64

Beginnings

A fresh page is like
a cool, crisp, clean sheet
ready to receive my dreams.

I Wanted

I wanted to be a Teenager
in pin curls, penny loafers with bobby sox
and my father's shirttail hanging out
from my dungarees rolled up above my knees.
Another Penny by Haenigsen*.

I'd be popular with lots of friends,
I'd have dates, be home by 10.

      But I missed it.

Oh, I had penny loafers with bobby sox
and my father's shirttail hanging out.
I had pin curls, friends and dates.
      And
I had pimples, cramps, homework,
      and insomnia.

So I wanted to be a grownup
with a permanent wave,
high-heeled shoes, nylons, gloves and a hat,
I'd buy fine clothes from Bendel's, Bonwits and Bergdorfs,
      another Paulette Goddard.

I'd go to the office, to cocktail parties,
listen to sophisticated syncopated jazz
and stay out all night with glamorous lovers.

But I missed it.

High heels hurt, my garter belt pinched, nylons itched,
I couldn't afford Bonwit's, Bergdorf's, or even Macy's Basement,
permanents fried my hair

    And
    I hated cocktail parties.

I married an available lover,
had a diamond ring, a honeymoon,
drove a station wagon in the suburbs,
wore slinky lingerie

    And maternity clothes.

I switched from cocktail parties to the PTA.
I was ready to retire.

Sleeping late every day I'd let my hair go where it would.
I'd wear sandals, long-hippy skirts, sunglasses.
I'd be imperious, mysterious and wild.

I'd go to the beach, to the mountains,
travel to faraway places,
go to lingering lunches,
learn Spanish, cook with sauterne and dance.

    But I missed it.

My eyes open wide at 5 a.m.
I gulp hormones, blood pressure pills, vitamins,
sandals hurt and I trip on long skirts.
Travel's too costly, the beach too hot, the
mountains too far, instead it's
trips to the doctor and dentist for me.
    But
I wear shorts, sneakers, and t-shirts
my hair runs wild
and it's certainly mysterious.

▶

I go to matinees and early-bird specials with friends.
We shop, visit art museums when nobody's there
and take all sorts of courses.

I watch sunrise on the lake, clouds in the sky
       and
I never go to cocktail parties.

Haenigsen was a cartoonist who drew "Penny" for the Herald Tribune in the 1940s. Penelope Millicent Pringle was the ideal teenager at the time.

Beach Walk

Five a.m.
just this side of drunken sleep
I deal from my soul and escape to the clouds
fog veils images of bench and streetlight
I fill with primordial
rotted fish-seaweed-beach chowder
cloud and bloom combine with ocean spray
I am spicy-sweet.

Soon sun burns off fog
birds chirp, gulls circle
a biker waves away my privacy
my energy rises
ideas begin to swirl in my mind
I think I am coming down with a poem.

Learning Jazzercise®

One, two, pivot swivel
forward back reach.
Reach swivel
step out step *huh?*

Kick ball change, ball change.

Right over left
left over right
chassè chassè.

Okay, okay
Hmmmm.

One, two pivot swivel
forward back
    damn
right over left
left over
    twist   down
    oops
think I'm bruised.

One, two pivot swivel
forward back reach.
Reach swivel
step out, step back
kick ball change, ball change
right over left
left over right
chassè chasse.

Okay, okay.

Got it?
  Maybe   not.

Ethiopian Princess

I am an Ethiopian Princess, you say
       hips swinging
       long skirt swaying
       jewelry chiming
       sandaled feet dancing
       spirits flying to the moon.
I'm not a princess, I respond
I am a woman well-loved.

On learning that I am an introvert

I forgive myself
for all the years of
failing miserably at activities
I absolutely loathed

GramIrene
Honoring lost women who hid their talents for proper domesticity

Summer routine at Lake Luzerne
breathing crisp, pine-infused mountain air
you paint

a dab of black brings shadow
and soil to the back of the white smock
on the girl in the foreground
and to the shirt that you wear
as you face your canvas
to paint the girls who face
their canvas, smearing yellow flowers.

A drip of green hits the floor,
you're dotted with red and blue
a patriotic salute to art perhaps.
Dab, smear, drip
lunch forgotten you lean toward the
easel   intent
      content.

You stop, sigh and pack the easel
put the art supplies back in the shed
scour the kitchen, bathroom
sweep, dust, make quick fixes
make his bed.

Week end

Cooking aromas chase away the fresh Adirondack breezes

▶

He sits in the sun reading *The New York Times* and
The Wall Street Journal while you prepare
coffee, eggs and toast and sandwiches with
kosher salami on rye bread
chopped liver on braided challah
chicken soup, braised beef brisket
swimming in onions, natural gravy,
roasted potatoes.
And always a can of Dr. Brown's soda to drink.

He returns to the city
you realize
you forgot to tell him
that you sold two paintings.

Mother

Ice cubes clinking
cigarette smoke stinking
in a bourbon drenched
Kent filtered cloud
she grasps a Kleenex crumble
reclines against her
headboard-throne and
barks orders.

Forgiving Mother

When I recall her face I
    no longer see my
    hopeless self
reflected in her gaze.

I see beyond hateful eyes into
    the ever-raveling
    sinkhole of hurt
that drove her.

Mother, forever acting out.
I just got in the way.

Teddie's Ashes

Teddie's Ashes were divided in half
or so we thought
Teddie was split in two equal parts
more or less
Teddie's ashes in two equal parts, more or less,
were put on the floor of my car and
half of Teddie was scattered in the Gulf
half of Teddie was scattered in North Carolina
but some of Teddie remained in that car
and I traded it in.

Part of Teddie floats free in the warm salty Gulf
part of Teddie flies wild in the mountain wind
and part of Teddie is stuck in that car
boogieing down the road perhaps
basso booming acid rock mocking his critic's ear
and Teddie won't have it.
How do you spoze he handles that?

Summer in the Hamptons

My toes grind on cold, damp sandy sheets
the Ocean rebounds in my mind fueling panic
that the waves will overcome us
to pound us to drown us
and shatter the plate-glass walls
of the main house
which is locked.

My sister and I share a tent in the sand.
With facilities unavailable
the beach plum bushes shine in the moonlight.

Split

Stuck at camp where I don't want to be
Hiking in the woods with no place to pee

My soft down pillow was left at home
All I have is a slab of foam

Shoot arrows, swim, run the track
I don't know if I'll ever get back

Arts and crafts, modern dance
That may be my only chance
       at sanity

A schedule in summer
Is really a bummer but

They had to get rid of me of course
So they could work out their divorce.

Maternal Lament

You're grieving
that's natural

lean into it as you'd
lean into a dance partner
sway with it, let it surround you.

Massage your grief
like you would a sore muscle
work with it.

      You won't be free if you don't.

He knows that
he calls to control you.

      Hang up that phone.

I know you love him, but
it's not about him.
it's about you.

Go for a walk
eat an ice cream cone
go shopping
go to Bath and Body Works for scents.

Fill the tub with hot, steamy
Tropical Passion Fruit bubbles
run your loofah all over that
adorable body of yours
possess it   for
it belongs to you.

Wrap yourself in a soft bath sheet
write him a note in the steam on the mirror.

    Make sure it's nasty.

And if you find yourself reaching
for the phone
          make sure you are calling me.

A Haiku for you two

A thrush or thrasher
baby bird with speckled breast
it too flew away

High Noon

Quell the longing in my soul
My own Gary Cooper so long gone
High Noon
The Sheriff so delighted by his bride
Contented smile
Hugging
Close
Each bound in the other's arms
No words.

I couldn't take the silences of my own Gary Cooper
I wasn't secure
Perhaps I'll never be
I miss him, my Gary Cooper
But I don't want the hurt.

Can I reunite with the Jewish Prince?
Rebuild?

Sex?
That too
With him?

Then which one?
Which way?

The center of sadness is out of control
Angst, longing,
Anxiety, sadness
Kill me

Leave me alone
Go away
Come back
I want someone to cherish me
Never happen
So OK
Gary Cooper let's try again

August 18

August 18 was your birthday
it rolled by unnoticed.
But was that the day I gathered

three wedding bands,
pendants and bracelets,
a panda ring, your class ring,
a charm bracelet dangling
symbols of your achievements
 with a miniature key
 to the City of Miami
and

melted them for cold, hard cash?
even the chains, clasps and spring rings

melted down on August 18, perhaps.

Happy Birthday.

Big Bird
Alice Cutts Wainwright
1908 – 1991

She pulled on loose trousers, boots,
a waterproof jacket
topped by a squashed rain hat
an androgynous general
summoned her Tropical Audubon troops
and marched into a South Dade tomato field
barking orders to us
a dead robin dangled from her gloved hand.

We fanned out.

Discovery: Open, empty pesticide cans in the field
Discovery: Open empty pesticide cans at an airstrip
Discovery: A witness to aerial spraying
          all suspicious.

A propeller mechanic in World War II
widowed and single mother
in reduced circumstances
she was among the first women to
enter law school and to
open a practice

First woman on the Miami Commission
she became vice mayor and
plowed her way into a man's world
relishing politics, national, state and local
lobbied against highway billboards, urban growth
a jetport in the Everglades
for the Garden Club and Audubon.

Ten thousand robins died that day
a hearing before the EPA led to
a ban on the pesticide by the State of Florida
          another job well done.

A Letter From Karen

I make my way
along spiked Y's that could be J's,
through flattened humps - - an M perhaps
beside rounded vowels
squashed together
sometimes on top of each other
tumbling down the page.

"We are well, the flowers are - -
A slams into N as if
the T E D had come
to a sudden stop
I decipher "planted."

This letter from Karen
slows me down like no E-mail.
I master each letter, one at a time
each word a victory.
I reread
savoring word and sentence.
        Karen, I miss you.

Leaving Fred

The top drawer once held old wallets
a jewelry case with cufflinks
abandoned since he retired.
The next drawer held shorts,
socks and tees, neatly folded.
Now, just another empty dresser
its loaded on a truck
bound for Goodwill.
A new life ahead.

She's moving to Minnesota
everything must go
the sofa, chairs, desks and beds.
The cherry valet stand
that held his suit ready for work
goes to a neighbor,
the hospital bed where he breathed his last
goes to Hospice House.
Even Mama's rocking chair finds a new home.

The house is empty
nothing left but shades of
two souls coupled.

Beyond tears, her bones ache,
feet drag from room-to-room
I realize that the move
is another death

she's leaving Fred behind.

Leaving For a Meeting

I'd better take it just in case I need it
then if I need it I will be so glad I brought it
but I shouldn't need it and
if I don't take it I won't waste time
wading through what I don't need
never to find what I am looking for.

And
if I know I didn't take it
I'll know I don't have it
then I won't look for it
and that will lighten my load

The Garden

Basket over her arm
she entered the garden
to snip snapdragons, gladiolas
dahlias and zinnias

to decorate the living room and
make a centerpiece for
the dining room table.

Looking around at the flowers
and vegetables
she noticed that once again
the chives were nibbled clean.

Her gaze hit the back fence
the rough, sharp chain link
shielded her from
the laborers on Second Street.

A premonition
she watched concrete overtake
the flowers
the vegetables
the lawn
knocking down the swings
and jungle gym

a relentless tide
covering her dreams
with parking lot reality.

The Last Gas Station

I drive down Hwy 17-92
the Purple Porpoise Restaurant
and Ranch Motel are
replaced by a gaping hole, a
Publix Market, Starbuck's and Quiznos.

The Linc Inn bar is now a Walgreens and the
church, a faux retro-style shopping strip.
Goodings market is about to be a mega condo.

At the last gas station
a young man
pumped my gas
cleaned the windshield and
checked under the hood.
If I had a problem
a mechanic was on hand.
Now it's a hole in the ground
soon to be a monster
apartment-shopping complex.
I've moved to a new town
without leaving home.

I Stopped at Athena for a Hummus/Taboule Pita

I dive in to chickpea-tahini hummus
the real thing, no slimy
modified corn starch to hold it together.
The perfect blend with
a touch of cumin mixed with the
crunch of lettuce-parsley-wheat germ
onion-tomato with lemon-mint tang
wrapped in a giant chewy pita
so big it takes two hands.
Lemon dribbles down my chin.
Got to eat it at home
        alone
            because I bathe in it.

The Train

Beyond city lights and glare
towers, taxis and the shops
is empty land that time forgot.
A train hurls by, it's barely there

yet it's a camera taking shots
of the passing littered yards
that contain the modern shards
of our indigenous burial plots.

Rejected by the second hands
a rusting car, a sofa thrown
tools, a toilet, a dog chews a bone
all skeletons gleaming in the sands.

A woman before her tar-paper shack
squinting in the sun's cruel blaze
hangs laundry in the diesel haze
which leaves a smudge, a streak of black.

Her rages, glows and hope
inured to the solid smack
of the train along the track
are forgotten in the engine's smoke.

Watching from my seat I'm bracing
just a speck much like a fly
I see the lives go hurtling by
as the train is racing
      Relentlessly.

Faith

I have faith that walking in the morning raises my spirits
that it won't rain while I'm walking and
I have faith that paintings color my world
music kneads my sprit,
sets my style, and adjusts my energy level
                just so
                as needed
and that Bach will massage my soul in
                times of sorrow and pain.

I have faith that the car will start, the garage door will close
I'll find parking at the office
that I won't get stuck in the elevator.
Yes! I do have faith that the elevator will work.
                and that's a lot of faith.

So I have faith in engineers, artists and musicians.
Perhaps that is faith in a larger power.

My faith is renewed as deep in the woods I
 worship in a cathedral
surrounded by dark green trees,
weeds, birds, bugs and breezes.
Even vultures and bats herald good luck.
All confirmed by rainbows.
Yes, rainbows.
I have faith in all that.

I'll Probably die in Florida
Inspired by "Black SUV" by Tony Hoagland

I'll probably die in Florida
but not on a Wednesday
that's my Jazzercize® day.

Perhaps I'll die on Tuesday
    my free day
I write all day
and it's garbage day.
Tuesday will be better.

Yes, I'll definitely die in Florida
on a Tuesday.

I'll sit at the computer in my
condo at the corner of
Woodridge and Goodridge
stuck in the middle of a poem
sick of Spider solitaire
marbled silk soy coffee blend
steaming by my side
not giving inspiration.
I'll look out the window
at the dog walkers strolling by
All of us ready for a new reality.

When I am gone

When I am gone
Divide my bones in two
a tibia, fibula
radius and ulna.
String them on silver threads
a wind chime
for each girl
so I can sing and dance
forever in the breezes.

The Wall

Blue cornflowers scattered in a yellow field
exhale stripper-soaked fumes.
A corner curl of attitude gives way
to reveal coils of anger.
Peel off ribbons of pride.
Another edge is stuck
more stripper
more scraping
beneath the anger
Fear.
The air is stripper saturated dizzy
wet-fear-mush disintegrates
to little scraps and crumbles.
The last chunks of fear-clutched-blue cornflowers
fall to the floor.
What now   courage?

Grieving Judy

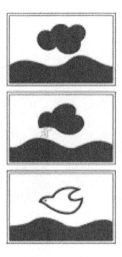

Author's Comments

This is a collection of essays and poetry written before, during and after the final illness and death of my sister. Her care circle and I prepared a book, _Honoring Judith Rosenberg,_ in 2016 which raised funds for Austin Tan Cerca. It included her writings, and art, as well as poems and essays from her family and friends.

This is my grieving which continues. It includes poetry and essays, some critiqued and some not.

I give thanks to Teresa L. Bruce, who polished the first go around, and to Joyce Haggerty who gave it a final peek; and to my poetry colleagues in Florida State Poets and to my family.

Farewell

Fifteen Days in February-March 2015

Trapped in Austin at Cindy's "Wild Hare," a mini-farm of friend-tenants' cottages cozied among flower beds, herbs, a struggling peach tree, and free-range chickens ... I wait.

I sleep in Judy's bed, walk her dog, arrange her things.

Judy sleeps all the time. Morphine eases assisted breathing. Her care circle, the real family, ever in attendance for two years, refuses to pull the plug. I lurk in the shadows.

> We continue
> separate paths
> I wait for tears that
> never come.

Dazed, abandoned among boxes of her photos, I pack up her clothing and vials of pills with child-resistant caps strewn around her room and her bathroom.

Alone.
Numb.

Reading Alice Munro

I am reading *Dear Life Stories*
by Alice Munro
my sister's book split
by book marks scribbled
with comments
"Original perception corrected"
"Joke—naïve"
I cherish it
so Judy.

I hug it to me
can't hug her
she's in ICU.

I'm looking around her bedroom
lusting
what do I want to take?
She'll never know.

Framed cartoons and drawings
by her own pens and brushes
mingle with family photos
to scamper around the walls.

Hand-woven fair-trade scarves and a
quilt made by a friend
are casually thrown on a chair,
a ceramic mug sits on the bookcase next to
a basket of her creation filled with mail.

Beyond knick-knack status
they're all special
so Judy.

I want it all
left as it is.

Overwhelmed by the energy, the social action, and the spirituality of her St. Hildegarde's and Austin Tan Cerca de la Frontera communities I observe them celebrate their Judith, a happy, passionate, brilliant activist, writer, musician. One talks about her courage facing border guards when taking delegations to the maquiladora factories in Piedras Negras, Mexico. Another celebrates her music, her writing. They clog her hospital room in reverence and come to her house to go through her things. I rescue a family Bible walking out the door.

What I Remember
a haibun

The story goes
that we danced with joy at the edge of the sea, the musty tide raced in bringing briny foamy bits and pieces of shells, marine worms, seaweed; dead and dying fish. We taunted seagulls, sandpipers and each other. I remember running through the dunes our shins wind whipped by beach grass, bare feet sliced by shells, pebbles and occasionally by broken glass.

What really happened?
We danced by the sea in anger and loneliness, locked ourselves in our own rooms, my sister and I. We followed our differences. Me with my movie stars scrapbooks, she with her model cars shuddering at the smashing surf that inhabits us still.

>Thunderous waves wash
>detritus on our shore
>emotion left behind

I see Judy, barefoot, in dungarees, braids flying, running through the dunes in East Hampton, trespassing in the mansions that lined the beach. I won't trespass. She calls me a " 'fraidy cat", rails at my timidity. I quake at her temper.

Judy hides under her bed and trips people as they walk by.

When older, she wanders the streets of New York City at night rather sequester in our New York apartment to feed from a case of hash our parents left for our dinner. Judy cuts herself with a shard from a glass she has smashed. I am her older sister; I try to take care of her. She rejects my comfort.

‡

A zombie breathing through a tube in her throat, her eyes flutter, disengaged despite the music and the poetry we read to her. Someone is with her all day and night. I take shifts, make final arrangements.

Mary brings a guitar and sings hymns.

Brigitte brings a thermos of hot ginger tea which fills the room with comforting aromas.

Geoff brings roses, which must be hidden from the nurses.

"She smiled when I told her you were here." ~ ~ Harriet

"She looks serene, just like my mother did when she was dying." ~ ~ Brigitte turns the bed to face the sun streaming in through the window.

"She's glowing." ~ ~ Tina.

"Oh, you're her sister. Judith told me you're not intellectual." ~ ~Brenda.

I am here but not present.

> And I the sister
> who officially loves her
> still struggling to
> define us
> to define me
> as she lies comatose
> her feet blue and about
> to explode ▶

Kim brings stalks of rosemary, butterfly bush, acanthus, viburnum, covering her with weeds and dirt "to ease her transition."

I try to feel Judy's spirit but I just see coma in a pile of dirt.

‡

It is done. She is dead. I walk around her bed. She's still covered with weeds but stone cold, and I'm still disappointed that I don't feel her spirit dancing around me. The nurse unhooks oxygen and straightens the bed stand. People stream in, crying, texting, while I fight a home viewing with Judy packed in ice like an oyster on the half shell. The hospital scene is enough.

I prevail.

At last acknowledged, I am family.

And Beyond

Fed Ex delivers boxes from Austin. Oil paintings, correspondence, lots of photos and copies of bank statements, tax statements, and death certificates have arrived in Florida. I will never go to Austin again. Grief lingers. I hang Judy's pictures and buy a new file cabinet.

The papers show a life I never knew. Pictures of Judy, a professional in New York City, a daughter hamming it up for the camera with Daddy, drawings of her working world crammed into a file with photos of family occasions I never knew about.

I see that when I moved to Florida I was erased.

Toward the end of Judy's life we visited each other, trying to make a relationship. I went to Austin for holidays, took her to chemo and radiation. We went folk dancing and attended an open mic where she insisted I read, showing me off to her Austin friends.

Judy came to Florida on New Year's 2013 bringing medical paraphernalia to drain a fluid buildup in her lungs. We walked around Lake Lily, went to the movies, and sang the entire score of *Guys and Dolls* at a New Year's Eve party.

But I was trapped in a gutter of the past and couldn't connect.

Drums of childhood echo
I'm not who I might be as

My feet follow the tribal dance.

▶

The care circle honored Judith's humor, passions, and intellect. I didn't know their new Judith. I knew the angry Judy, the "Tuffin." I struggled against an oppression prompted by Judy's anger and the depression I couldn't define. I cowered, before her
strength and her courage, for she tried everything. I lived in the shadow of her accomplishments. Judy played the trumpet and guitar, harvested reeds to make baskets, mastered the unicycle — got a Ph.D.! She was everything I wasn't, and when I began to write and find my voice, she validated me, but she too took up a pen and was better . . . I thought. I remain intimidated.

Heaven in Travis County

O, how I in pin-curled ringlets
tried to nurture you, care for you,

the tough one
in jeans, boots and a
sailor's cap your braids dangling.
You stomped your way through
parental barbs and neglect.

So you found paradise but
God said it's time you found me.

A fractious bird who tried to escape your
Churckendoosian differentness,
a refugee from
hostile family members
you found heaven in
Travis County, Texas.
     Imagine that!

In the ultra-con, neo-con heartland,
hardly heaven for a Churckendoose,
you found Jesus, praise be, and
built communities where
everyone fit — no one an outcast.

Surrounded by multi-colored
multi-gendered-lingual
tribes of loving   you danced,
you sang, made art and music,
became silly, and prayed
with those cast out of the heartland.

▶

And at the apex of your delight
God said, "Come join me"
and you left us all behind.

Why did His invitation come
just when you had found heaven on earth?

Part chicken, turkey, duck, and goose, Churckendoose talks in rhyme and can't walk. He tap dances. The 1947 book and recording by Ben Ross Berenberg and Ray Bolger taught that differences can be a very good thing.

May 29, 2015

We walk around the lake,
my sister and I.
A half cup of her is snuggled
deep in her woven blue purse
hanging around my neck.

Three p.m.
it's time   and
while the rest of her,
mixed with the ashes of her dog, Chela,
blows gently into the Rio Grande
we in Florida are doing our part.

The half cup of Judy
blows into Lake Lily and
onto my slacks, shoes and
even my face.

It's a sunny day.
Thankfully few people
see me toss those ashes,
trip on a tree root, nearly heaving myself
into the yucky muck.

It's amazing how a large engine of a
woman was reduced to soft dust to
float in the wind, blow into Lake Lily
into the Rio Grande.

Winner of Honorable Mention in 2020 Thomas Burnett Swann
Poetry Prize Competition, and published in Revelry 2020

Judy's Ashes

Five feet six of vibrant
dancing, singing, praying woman
organizier of communities of
family, protestors, educators, artists, and writers
compressed into a
sack of ashes that
fit into a plastic bag from the grocery store.

Packets of people
have a half cup of Judy.

She's scattered in the Rio Grande at the border,
in Lake Lily in Maitland, Florida,
and now I find some of her
will rest in Cindy's garden and
didn't St. Hilde's get a half cup?

With all our little shares
She measures up to much more
than a plastic grocery bag.

And More Poems

Lake Lily

What is that?
It's a Muscovy
Don't you remember them
from Louse Point?
My sister didn't.

She was getting on my nerves.
We wanted to take a walk and
I was sick of the neighborhood.

Is that an egret?
No, it's an ibis,
see the decurved bill?
I didn't remember them around
when I first moved here.

It was four p.m. and I hoped
we wouldn't meet anyone
I needed silence.
As we walked along
I began to absorb my lake.
She nodded at another bird.
A limpkin, I said.
I didn't remember limpkins
around here either
but it sure looked like one.

I explained coots and
gallinules and
told her if we were lucky
we might see a purple one.

My sister visited for fifteen days.
We never had been close
and I'm a loner.
I gave her my bedroom, my bathroom,
she brewed her stinky tea,
critiqued my poems and
when things got tense:

Let's walk around the lake.

Again? Yes again
around and around
admiring birds, finding turtles, petting dogs

She's gone back to Texas
but I feel a sense of loss
when I walk around Lake Lily.

Chucho

Chucho is flat on the floor
legs in four directions
cooling his tummy
staring expectantly.
Part champagne poodle, part Airedale,
his compact body sits
atop long legs—very long legs.

She called him "my hero."
I didn't find a hero,
just a trickster
sneaking out to give chase,
borrowing shoes and
when neglected,
he might have marked a pillow.

When I cleaned out her things
Chucho became an appendage
exchanging love and comfort.

‡

Storm Warning

I feel dark clouds form
a low-barometer headache

lightning precedes the
thunder news clash
I blow to Texas in
spiral rain bands

to your bedside
with your helper bees
buzzing around
advising, guiding
feeding me in gales of
hundred-mile winds

I am buffeted by debris
of a life well lived
by a person I never knew
by our harsh words past
mom always loved you best
my baby sister
spinning down the vortex

the eye passes over
a dead calm
I meditate

eye-wall winds pick up
bees keening demand
a viewing but
    I am done
for me it is over.

April 21, 2015
a kyrielle

Play with the angels in the sky
Dance and sing now you can fly
And eat ripe olives all day long
You're in a place where you belong

The place in heaven is all set
You'll organize something, I'll bet
Your talents will never leave you
Art, music, writing still please you

Happy birthday, my sister dear,
I really wish you could be here
And miss you so, I will be strong
You're in a place where you belong.

Hoodeet

Scattered
she swims with turtles and ducks
on algal waters
flies through moss-draped trees
to dance with stars and
here lies Hoodeet
a hole in my heart
which longs for
reparations of
opportunities missed.

Alienation

Gone all the years
from the stylish New York family
which moved on without me, a
Florida housewife, mother, activist,
administrator, student,
journalist-poet -writer
I'm an outsider again.

I think of myself not a Friedman,
which is who I am, but
as Allie, a troubling piece
struggling to fit into the
Rosenberg puzzle
which is gone now
that Judy has died
and left a chasm of alienation.

Made in the USA
Monee, IL
23 July 2021